Crystal Recipes

Rinku Patel

Copyright

© 2018, Acorn Gecko SRL

ALL RIGHTS RESERVED. This book contains material protected under International and Federal Copyright Laws and Treaties. Any unauthorized reprint or use of this material is prohibited. No part of this book may be reproduced or transmitted in any form or by any means, electronic or mechanical, including photocopying, recording, or by any information storage and retrieval system without express written permission from the publisher.

Table of Contents

Introduction 5
Cleansing Crystals 7
Charging the Crystals 11
Programming Crystals 13
How to Use Crystals 17
Crystals ailment recipes A 21
Crystals ailment recipes B 26
Crystals ailment recipes C 30
Crystals ailment recipes D 35
Crystals ailment recipes E 38
Crystals ailment recipes F 41
Crystals ailment recipes G 44
Crystals ailment recipes H 46
Crystals ailment recipes I 50
Crystals ailment recipes J 53
Crystals ailment recipes K 54
Crystals ailment recipes L 55
Crystals ailment recipes M 57
Crystals ailment recipes N 61
Crystals ailment recipes O 63
Crystals ailment recipes P 65
Crystals ailment recipes R 69
Crystals ailment recipes S 71

Crystals ailment recipes T 76
Crystals ailment recipes U 79
Crystals ailment recipes V 81
Crystals ailment recipes W 83
Zodiacs and Crystals 85
Beauty Combo..88
Elemental Crystals 90
Crystals for Soon to Be Moms and New Moms 92
Crystals for Furry Babies – Pets..95
Top 12 97
Chakras and Crystals..105
About the Author...107

Introduction

First things first, like any other spiritual or alternative healing modality, crystal healing requires immense faith and strong intention.

You need to have faith that the crystal will take your wishes to the Universe and that they will be manifested no matter what. You cannot use crystals for evil intentions or to harm others.

Before using crystals make sure they are cleansed and de-attuned off their previous energies. After cleansing, you need to charge your program with Reiki, mantra, prayer or any other divine energy you know.

Next is crystal programming. This is done to direct energy towards a specific goal. As you read ahead, you'll find a brief guidance about cleansing, charging, programming and using crystal combinations.

This book is about combining various crystals for ailments and other issues. You don't need all the crystals specified in the list, these are just options for you to choose from.

Go with the stones you already have or the ones that are resonating with you. Combining various crystals will optimize the energies of the crystal combo and adding Clear Quartz to any combination amplifies the energy of all the other crystals.

Listed in the combinations are the crystals that are easily available. You can add stones of your choice in any given combinations.

These are not ALL the stones used for the particular ailments, listed are only a few of them that could help. I have mentioned stones that are easily available and affordable to all.

You don't need to have hundreds of crystals to heal yourself or others, a few right ones are good enough. This book will guide you to work with a few selected stones to heal various issues.

If you make any elixir, make sure that the crystals you are using are safe and not toxic. In case of toxin crystals like Pyrite, Lapis Lazuli, Moldavite, Malachite etc, surround your crystals in a container, do not put them directly in water.

Cleansing Crystals

Having bought your crystals, next thing is to take care of them. Cleansing crystals is the most important thing to do before a healing session, setting a grid or programming for any other use.

Those who are new to crystals may start wondering why crystals need cleansing. I asked my hubby to give me his crystal pendant to cleanse. He said, "no its ok, it is not dirty☺".

Actually, crystals tend to absorb the energies around them. To diffuse the accumulated negative energy, we need to cleanse them. Cleansing removes all the previous programming too. So once cleansed, charge and program your crystals.

Let us explore a few crystal cleansing methods here:

Salt Water- Add salt to water and soak crystals for 4-5 hours in salt water. Not all crystals resonate with salt and water, so check before soaking them.

Running Water- Hold your crystal under a tap, stream or any form of fresh running water. Imagine all the accumulated negative energy flowing away with running water.

Earth- Place your crystals back to their original cradle. Bury your crystals in your garden, planter or backyard. Alternatively, gather some soil in a container and bury your crystal. After removing, wipe it clean and make sure no soil particles are left.

Dry Salt- Place your crystals in a bowl of dry sea salt/rock salt/Himalayan salt. Make sure there are no leftover salt particles once you are done cleansing.

Breathe- Hold your crystal in your palm and blow forcefully on it. Imagine you are blowing a white light over your crystals. Keep blowing till you feel your crystal is shiny or simply blow thrice with the intention to cleanse.

Flame- Just rotate your crystal 7 times over a candle flame to cleanse it. You can even pass your crystal quickly through flame.

Moon/Sun- This is one of the simplest and safest method. Simply leave your crystals out in sunlight or moon light. Not all crystals resonate with sunlight so please check crystal's properties before placing in sunlight.

Smudging- Use sage or incense stick to cleanse the crystal. Simply pass your crystal through sage/incense stick smoke.

Reiki- Hold crystal in your palm and draw the power symbol, give Reiki with the intention to remove negative energy from the crystal.

Bell or Singing Bowl- The vibration of the bell or the singing bowl has the power to cleanse your crystals. Just play the sound of bell/singing bowl near the crystals.

Selenite/Citrine/Carnelian- Selenite is considered a 'Universal Stone Cleaner'. It does not need cleansing. Even Citrine and Carnelian have the properties to cleanse other crystals. Simply place your crystal over any of these clusters or add tumbles with your crystal. Alternatively, put all crystals in a box and program your stones to cleanse all crystals in the box.

Beach- Going to a beach? Take your crystal along and cleanse with sea water.

Pendulum- Program your pendulum to cleanse the crystal and hold it over the one you want to cleanse.

Third Eye- Direct white light on your crystals using your third eye with the set intention.

Crystal Clusters/Geode- Some crystals (citrine, carnelian, selenite) don't need frequent cleansing. They can be used to cleanse other crystals too. Simply place your crystals on the geode or cluster.

Plants- Lay your crystal besides your favorite flower or plant. Plants have the natural ability to transmute negative energy into positive energy.

Pyramid dome- The shape of a pyramid itself is very powerful. Place your crystals under the pyramid dome and they will be cleansed from any accumulated negative energy.

Flower essence- Soak flower petals of any flower in water for a few hours. Fill this water in a spray bottle and spray on crystals.

Charging the Crystals

Between cleansing and programming crystals, there is one other step to do and that is charging the crystals. Charging the crystals means infusing them with Divine energies. Those who know Reiki usually charge them by giving Reiki to crystals. They program and charge simultaneously. But what about those who are not attuned to Reiki?

Below are a few steps to charge your crystals with Divine energies.

1. Draw Cho Ku Rei or Dai Ko Myo or any other symbol you are guided to on your stone. State your intention to infuse the stone with Reiki energy and let the energy flow for about 5 minutes. You can also state your intention to program for particular issue and give Reiki simultaneously.

2. Prayers- You can charge your crystals with any prayer of any God/Angels you resonate with. Hold the crystal in your palms and state - "I dedicate this crystal to the energies of _____ (God or Angel name) and ask them to infuse the crystal with Divine energies". You can say any other prayer if you wish.

3. Mantras- Like prayers, you can infuse your crystals with mantras energies. Either you can infuse with any mantra or opt for a mantra that resonates with your wish. Hold the stones in your palm and chant the chosen mantra 108 times.
4. Make angelic grid to charge your stones with angelic energies.
5. Place outside in yard, garden or balcony on a full moon night to infuse your crystal with divine moon energies.
6. Rotate over candle flame to infuse the stone with the fire element.

Personally, I do not follow any one particular method. I just do as my intuition guides me. At times I charge with Reiki, at times with prayers or at times with mantras. The angelic grid works best when you have multiple stones to charge.

So before programming your stones, don't forget to infuse them with Divine energies.

Programming Crystals

What is crystal programming?

When you program a crystal, you are actually storing your intention and your energy in that crystal. Your crystal can be programmed for any intention and wish, just make sure that the crystal's properties resonate with your wish. When I say you can program your crystal for any intention, I do not mean that you can program it to harm others. It will not work because, just like Reiki, crystals also can only be used for a person's highest good.

Why do we need to program the crystal?

Crystals have their own healing properties which work regardless of them being programmed or not. By programming, you are putting your intention into the crystal, which is then carried to the Universe resulting the outcome in a magnificent way. Select that crystal that resonates with your wish. When I place my bowl of assorted tumbles on my altar, I state my intention: *"May these crystals spread their energy according to all their healing properties to heal me and my family on all levels and for our highest good. May they absorb all impure energies and transmute them to light."* If I am programming a single stone for a specific intention or for a grid, then I program that crystal for that specific intention.

Will the programmed intention stay forever?

This is quite a debatable question. According to some people, crystals need programming every month or they lose it. Whereas including me, some say that once a crystal is programmed it can hold the intention for years and years or till you de-program it.

How to program the crystal?

Before programming any crystal, make sure that the crystal is cleansed of any impure energies and de-programmed of past energies and intentions. There are multiple ways to cleanse crystals.

Different ways to program crystals

Chanting the intention- Hold your cleansed crystal in your left palm and cover it with your right palm. State the intention aloud if possible, alternatively you can whisper or say it in your mind. Keep chanting your intention and stay focused, keeping all your attention and intention to the crystal. Suppose you need love, keep chanting 'Bring Love'. Keep that thought on and hold it for minimum 68 seconds. Repeat the process holding the crystal in your right hand.

Reiki charged- Hold a cleansed crystal in non-dominant hand, draw symbols and put dominant palm over the crystal and Reiki the crystal with your intention. Again, keep the thought for 68 seconds to make the manifestation faster.

Third eye- Take a cleansed crystal, hold it over your third eye, not touching the third eye. Beam white light from your third eye into the crystal. If you know Reiki, beam the power symbol and the master symbol into the crystal with the third eye. Think about your wish, imagine transferring your wish from your mind to the crystal. Envisage the desired outcome and place the crystal on your altar.

Tumbles together- If there are many crystals for general use, place all crystals together, draw symbols on them and give Reiki with the intention- *May these crystals spread their energy according to all their healing properties to heal me and my family on all levels and*

15

for our highest good. May they absorb all impure energies and transmute them to light.

Visualization- Hold crystal in your palms. Think about your wish, visualize it being fulfilled. Stay focused and keep visualizing your wish and desired outcome, your reaction to it and how you would feel about it. Keep visualizing the full scenario.

Breathe intention into crystal- Hold your crystal, be in a meditative state and stay focused on your wish. As above, visualize the desired outcome. Take your crystal near your mouth and blow with force on your stone transferring your wish to it.

How to Use Crystals

These crystal combinations can be used in various ways. For best effect select 3 or more stones to create your perfect combo. Do not make a clutter by adding too many stones.

- Put in purse, bag, wallet, laptop bag, school bag
- Put under pillow or mattress at night
- Program and place on altar or home temple

- Place in a particular room or office
- Gridding the bed
- Gridding the room or whole house
- Wear in jewelry form such as necklace, bracelet, anklet, pendant, earrings, ring…
- Make crystal water/elixir (Only nontoxic crystals for direct elixir)

- Place according to Feng Shui or Vastu location
- Put in drawers where you put cash and documents
- Keep inside manifesting box as per your wishes in the box
- Meditate with crystals
- Make crystal grids as per your issues
- Distant healing
- Distant healing with Reiki
- Carry with you in pockets or bra
- Place as a showpiece
- On bedside table
- Make coasters with chips
- As keychains
- As door hangers
- Make your pets wear
- Gift
- Weave in dream catchers
- Use crystal soaps
- Charge your food
- Use at work place for protection and harmony
- Cleanse other stones with self-cleansing stones
- Use with Reiki or other healing practices
- Chakra cleansing
- Use with tarot and oracle cards
- Charge cosmetics like shampoo, conditioner, creams, oils, lipsticks etc

*Note- Adding Clear Quartz to any of the combo amplifies the energies of other stones.

*Note- Some of the self-cleansing stones are Citrine, Carnelian and Selenite. Place these stones along with other crystals to keep them cleansed.

*Note- Make sure you always use cleansed and charged stones.

Crystals ailment recipes A
(Combine 3 or more crystals for best outcome)

ABANDONMENT- LOSS/GRIEF
Carnelian, Rose Quartz, Rhodonite

ABDOMINAL PROBLEM
Smoky Quartz, Calcite, Banded Agate, Blue Lace Agate, Garnet, Yellow Agate, Carnelian

ABUNDANCE
Citrine, Green Aventurine, Tiger's eye, Moss Agate, Ruby, Jade, Sunstone, Emerald, Malachite, Pyrite, Blue Tiger's eye, Red Tiger's eye, Cinnabar

ABUSE (VICTIM)
Ruby, Rhodonite, Obsidian, Ruby Obsidian,

ABUSIVE BEHAVIOR
Apache Tears, Carnelian, Lapis Lazuli, Rhodonite, Pink Calcite

ACCEPTANCE
Rose Quartz, Chyrsoprase, Pink Calcite, Blue Chalcedony, Blue Calcite, Aragonite, Tiger's eye, Rhodonite

ACCIDENT REDUCE
Amethyst, Carnelian, yellow Jasper, Snowflake Obsidian, Tiger's eye, Amethyst, Red Jasper, Malachite, Green Jasper, Fire Opal, Turquoise,

ACHES AND PAINS
Malachite, Blue Lace Agate, Lapis Lazuli, Yellow Agate, Banded Agate, Sunstone

ACNE
Amber, Amethyst, Aquamarine, Rose Quartz, Carnelian, Selenite

ADAPTATIONS
Amazonite, Turquoise, Chrysocolla, Bloodstone

ADDICTIONS
Amethyst, Amber, Carnelian, Hematite, Iolite, Kunzite, Sugilite, Hematite, Smoky Quartz, Red jasper

ADVENTURE
Sunstone, Malachite

AGGRESSIVENESS
Aquamarine, Rose Quartz, Amazonite

AKASHIC RECORDS ACCESS
Angelite, Mica, Moldavite, Selenite

ALCOHOL ABUSE
Black Onyx, Red Jasper

ALCOHOLISM
Amazonite, Amethyst, Red Jasper

ALLERGIES
Carnelian, Aquamarine, Turquoise, Rose quartz, Citrine, Yellow Calcite

ALLERGIES TO ANIMALS

Shungite, Poppy Jasper
ALIGNING CHAKRAS
Blue Kyanite
ALZHEIMERS
Lepidolite, Sodalite, Rose Quartz, Kunzite
AMBITION
Golden Rutile, Tiger's eye, Citrine, Pyrite
AMPLIFY ENERGY
Rutilated Quartz, Clear Quartz
ANAEMIA
Bloodstone, Hematite, Ruby, Red Jasper, Red Tiger's eye, Coral
ANGELIC COMMUNICATION
Angelite, Celestite, Selenite, Fuchsite, Amethyst, Celestite, Moldavite, Prehnite, Angel Aura Quartz, Herkimer Diamond, Danburite, Larimar
ANGER
Peridot, Amethyst, Blue Lace Agate, Rose Quartz, Kyanite, Moss Agate, Amazonite, Green Aventurine, Jade, Aquamarine
ANOREXIA
Carnelian, Orange Calcite
ANTI-AGING/AGEING
Rutilated Quartz, Rose Quartz, Sodalite, Kyanite, Rhodochrosite, Mookaite, Jade
ANXIETY
Green Aventurine, Mica, Amethyst, Orange Calcite, Lapis Lazuli, Black Onyx, Labradorite, Blue Tiger's eye, Turquoise, Chrysocolla, Blue Calcite, Azurite, and Malachite
APPRECIATION

Carnelian, Blue Lace Agate, Moldavite, Banded Agate, Lapis Lazuli, Iolite, Sodalite, Malachite

ARTHRITIS

Malachite, Blue Lace Agate, Banded Agate, Rhodonite, Carnelian, Azurite, Hematite, Black Tourmaline

ARTISTIC CREATIVITY

Amethyst, Purple Fluorite, Sugilite, Moss Agate, Carnelian

ASCENSION

Labradorite, Moldavite

ASTHMA

Malachite, Amber, Tiger's eye, Amethyst, Angelite, Lapis Lazuli, Rhodochrosite

ASTRAL TRAVEL

Ametrine, Angelite, Sapphire, Clear Quartz, Labradorite, Blue Tiger's Eye, Prehnite

ATTRACT ANGELS

Banded Agate, Blue Lace Agate, Celestite, Clear Quartz, White Agate

ATTRACT POSITIVE VIBRATIONS

Black Onyx

AURACOMBO-STABILIZE/PROTECT/STRENGTHEN/CLEANSE

Amazonite, Citrine, Labradorite, Clear Quartz, Sunstone, Celestite, Smoky Quartz, Sunstone, Jade, Green Fluorite

AURA CLEANING

Clear Quartz, Smoky Quartz, Green Fluorite, Black Kyanite, Labradorite

AURA HEALING

Strawberry Quartz

AURA PROTECT

Amethyst, Clear Quartz, Labradorite, Smoky Quartz

AURA REVITALIZE

Clear Quartz, Herkimer Diamond, Selenite, Moonstone, Rutilated Quartz

AUTISM

Sugilite, Moldavite, Sodalite, Lapis Lazuli, Amethyst

AUTOIMMUNE DISEASES

Rhodonite, Mookaite, Tantalite, Smoky Amethyst, Amethyst

AWARENESS INCREASE

Amethyst, Aquamarine, Bloodstone, Rhodochrosite

Crystals ailment recipes B
(Combine 3 or more crystals for best outcome)

BABY'S NURSERY

Rose Quartz, Amethyst, Selenite, Moonstone, Green Aventurine, Carnelian, Clear Quartz, Calcite, Hematite, Jade, Lapis Lazuli, Tiger's Eye

BACK PAIN

Carnelian, Hematite, Moss Agate, Selenite, Lapis lazuli, Clear Quartz, Calcite

BACTERIAL INFECTION

Shungite

BALANCE BLOOD SUGAR-

Mica, Chrysocolla, Pyrite, Citrine, Ruby, Bloodstone

BALANCE HORMONE

Moonstone, Watermelon, Tourmaline, Amethyst, Clear Quartz, Labradorite

BALANCE PHYSICAL BODY

Carnelian, Smoky Quartz, Snowflake Obsidian, Amazonite, Bloodstone, Tiger's eye

BEAUTY

Opal, Aquamarine, Rose Quartz, Amber, Jade, Rhodochrosite, Amethyst, Mookaite, Moonstone, Citrine, Green Onyx

BED WETTING (CHILD NEEDS EMOTIONAL SUPPORT)
Amazonite, Carnelian, Rose Quartz, Sodalite, Tiger's Eye
BED WETTING (CAUSE- STRESS)
Amethyst, Green Aventurine, Blue Lace Agate, Lapis lazuli, Black Tourmaline
BELIEFS
Lapis Lazuli, Snowflake Obsidian, Blue Apatite
BIPOLAR
Ruby, Red Jasper, Lepiodite, Bloodstone, Carnelian, Celestite, Fluorite, Tiger's eye, Kunzite
BLADDER
Amber, Aquamarine, Blue Tourmaline, Jade, Mookaite, Bloodstone, Rose Quartz, Fluorite, Aventurine, Red Jasper, Orange Calcite, Smoky Quartz
BLEEDING STOP
Bloodstone, Carnelian, Red Jasper, Sapphire, Ruby, Clear Quartz, Hematite
BLISTERS
Rose Quartz, Aquamarine, Blue Lace Agate, Selenite, Quartz
BLOATING
Zeolite, Zoisite, Citrine, Ocean Jasper
BLOCKAGES (self-imposed)
Larimar, Black Obsidian, Sugilite, Lapis Lazuli, Elestial Quartz
BLOOD CIRCULATION
Bloodstone, Carnelian, Ruby, Hematite, Garnet, Fancy Jasper, Copper, Amazonite
BLOOD CLOT

Bloodstone, Hematite, Orange Calcite, Rhodochrosite, Ruby, Amethyst

BLOOD PRESSURE HIGH

Sodalite, Green Aventurine, Green Tourmaline, Fuchsite, Ruby, Bloodstone, Lapis Lazuli

BLOOD PRESSURE LOW

Carnelian, Garnet, Red Jasper, Ruby, Any Tourmaline, Emerald, Chyrsoprase, Bloodstone, Malachite

BONE BROKEN

Hematite, Malachite, Howlite, Apatite, Fluorite, Pyrite

BONE HEALTH

Selenite, Pyrite, Calcite, Lapis Lazuli

BRAIN INJURY

Lapis, Aquamarine, Labradorite, Lapis Lazuli, Aqua Aura, Amazonite, Turquoise

BRAIN MELENOMA

Amber, Larimar, Sulphur, Amethyst, Rhodonite, Smoky Quartz, Clear Quartz, Hematite

BRAVERY

Ruby, Chyrsoprase, Aquamarine, Bloodstone

BREATHING PROBLEMS

Amorganite, Apophyllite, Moss Agate, Amber, Black Onyx

BROKEN HEART

Rhodonite, Rhodochrosite, Rose Quartz, Green Aventurine, Amazonite, Pink Tourmaline

BRONCHITIS

Rutilated Quartz, Pyrite, Amber, Peridot, Emerald

BRUISE

Rose Quartz, Amethyst, Blue Lace Agate, Fluorite, Hematite, Carnelian

BURNS

Rose Quartz, Sodalite, Amethyst, Clear Quartz, Rhodonite, Blue Lace Agate

BUSINESS COMBO

Carnelian- Confidence, Positive feeling, Motivation

Green Aventurine- Good luck, Brings new opportunities, Leadership

Moss Agate- Increase hope, Positive energy, Optimism, Self-esteem, Attract abundance

Amethyst- Clear thinking

Citrine- Money magnet

Tiger's Eye- Release blocked energy, Accomplish goals

Amazonite- For writers and artists (creativity)

Fluorite- Absorb new ideas

Lapis Lazuli- Public speech

Sodalite- Team work

Selenite- Peaceful atmosphere

Smoky Quartz- Protects from unwanted energies

Crystals ailment recipes C
(Combine 3 or more crystals for best outcome)

CALMING

Blue Lace Agate, Blue Calcite, Aquamarine, Amazonite, Moss Agate, Amethyst, Turquoise, Chrysocolla

CANCER TREATMENT SUPPORT

Sugilite, Amethyst, Smoky Quartz, Fluorite, Selenite, Green Tourmaline, Bloodstone, Azurite, Moonstone, Sodalite, Black Onyx, Peridot. Also, any crystal resonating with the affected chakra.

CAREER AND PROFESSION

Amethyst, Moonstone, Carnelian, Green Aventurine, Citrine, Tiger Eye, Moss Agate, Black Tourmaline, Pyrite, Botswana Agate, Honey Calcite, Malachite, Jade, Peridot, Ruby, Lepiodite

CENTERING

Smoky Quartz, Aragonite, Amethyst, Blue Lace Agate, Moldavite

CHANGE- (DEAL AND ACCEPT)

Prehnite, Pyromorphite, Lab, Angelite, Datolite

CHARM

Sunstone, Green Tourmaline, Orange Calcite, Rose Quartz, Pink Tourmaline

CHEMOTHERAPY
Smoky Quartz, Sugilite, Selenite, Citrine, Carnelian, Rose Quartz, Amethyst

CHICKEN POX
Pearl, Azurite, Malachite, Rose Quartz

CHILDREN COMBO
Tantrum- Amethyst
Night terror- Amethyst
Shy/timid children- Aventurine, Tiger's Eye
Acne- Carnelian
Low self-esteem- Carnelian
Unfocused- Clear Quartz
Hyperactive- Citrine
Hurt emotions- Rose Quartz
Aggressive- Rose Quartz
Sensitive- Jade
Daydream- Tiger's Eye

CHOLESTROL
Yellow Fluorite, Green Aventurine, Carnelian, Bloodstone

CHRONIC PAIN
Celestite, Lapis Lazuli, Amethyst, Clear Quartz, Carnelian, Copper, Garnet, Hematite, Gold, Kunzite, Turquoise, Malachite

CLAIRAUDIENCE
Mahogany Obsidian, Snowflake Obsidian, Angelite, Celestite, Lapis Lazuli, Amethyst, Apophyllite, Moldavite, Prehnite, Sodalite, Labradorite

CLAIRSENTIENCE

Amber, Angelite, Rutilated Quartz, Orange Kyanite, Labradorite, Vesuvianite, Blue Apatite, Sunstone, Pyrite

CLAIRVOYANCE

Blue Apatite, Herkimer Diamond, Labradorite, Tiger's eye, Moonstone, Pink Sapphire, Fuchsite, Rutilated Quartz, Topaz, red Tiger's eye, Blue Tiger's eye, Angelite, Amethyst, Sodalite, Celestite

CLARITY

Aquamarine, Celestite, Emerald, Lithium, Citrine, Rhodonite, Blue Lace Agate, Yellow Jasper, Yellow Aventurine

CLAUSTROPHOBIA

Green Aventurine, Green Tourmaline, Chrysoprase

COLIC

Garnet, Jade, Malachite, Blue Lace Agate, Rose Quartz, Amber, Yellow Aventurine

COMFORT

Carnelian, Citrine, Malachite, Rose Quartz, Azurite, Danburite, Peridot, Aquamarine, Any Aventurine

COMMITMENT (GIVE)

Rhodochrosite, Tiger's eye, Ruby, Pyrite

COMMON COLD

Fluorite, Carnelian, Moss Agate, Labradorite, Blue Lace Agate, Green Aventurine, Green Calcite

COMMUNICATION

Aquamarine, Blue Lace Agate, Turquoise, Lapis Lazuli, Kyanite, Amazonite, Blue Tiger's eye, Sodalite, Blue Tanzanite, Rhodonite, Petalite, Helidor, Citrine, Moss Agate

COMMUNICATION WITH HIGHER-SELF

Labradorite, Angelite, Blue Tiger's eye, Celestite, Moldavite, Prehnite, Fluorite

COMMUNICATION WITH SPIRIT

Lapis Lazuli, Kyanite, Angelite, Amethyst, Apophyllite, Selenite, Petrified Wood

COMPASSION

Lapis Lazuli, Sodalite, Angelite, Celestite, Rose Quartz

COMPUTER RADIATION

Hematite, Black Tourmaline, Smoky Quartz, Red Jasper, Black Obsidian, Shungite, Shieldite, Amazonite, Lepiodite

CONCENTRATION

Carnelian, Fluorite, Lapis Lazuli, Ruby, Hematite, Banded Agate, Calcite, Tiger's eye, Apophyllite, Danburite

CONFIDENCE

Carnelian, Citrine, Ruby, Rhodonite, Yellow Aventurine, Garnet, Green Tourmaline, Hematite, Lapis Lazuli, Rose Quartz, Red Tiger's eye, Fuchsite, Selenite, Jade

CONFLICT

Rose Quartz, Prehnite, Jade, Amber, Amazonite, Aventurine

CONNECT WITH HIGHER-SELF

Selenite, Ametrine, Jade

CONNECT WITH HIGHER-REALM

Moonstone, Moldavite, Jade, Angelite, Selenite, Blue Celestite, Prehnite

CONTROL (BALANCE)

Pietersite, Lemurian Seed, Citrine

CONSTIPATION

Red Jasper, Ruby, Fuchsite, Citrine, Any Fluorite

CORD CUTTING

Botswana Agate, Clear Quartz, Sunstone, Selenite, Rainbow Obsidian, Petalite

COUGH/CONGESTION

Amber, aquamarine, blue lace agate, rose quartz, blue Tiger's eye, azurite, malachite, topaz, copal

COURAGE

Bloodstone, Carnelian, Aquamarine, Ruby, Tiger's eye, Garnet, Hematite, Red Tiger's eye, Sunstone, Red Amethyst, Red Spinel, Ametrine, Apophyllite, Goldstone, Titanium Quartz, Pyrite+Black Tourmaline

CRAMPS

Turquoise, Malachite, Rose Quartz, Hematite, Smoky Quartz, Bloodstone, Chrysocolla, Lapis lazuli, Moonstone, Carnelian, Unakite, Garnet

CREATIVITY

Citrine, Green Aventurine, Carnelian, Amazonite, Rose Quartz, Sodalite, Moonstone, Pyrite, Aquamarine, Amethyst, Lapis Lazuli, Celestite, Ametrine, Green Tourmaline. (Put at your workplace for extra creativity)

CRITICAL ATTITUDE

Black Tourmaline, Lapis Lazuli

CRYING

Rose Quartz, Blue Lace Agate, White Agate

CURSE

Red Tiger's eye, Black Tourmaline, Tourminated Quartz

Crystals ailment recipes D
(Combine 3 or more crystals for best outcome)

DEAFNESS

Lapis Lazuli, Rhodonite, Blue Tourmaline, Green Tourmaline, Black Tourmaline, Snowflake Obsidian, Amethyst, Amber, Mahogany Obsidian

DECAY

Pearl, Ruby

DECISION MAKING

Amethyst, Citrine, Green Aventurine, Rainbow Fluorite, Jade, Ametrine, Azurite, Rutilated Quartz, Lepidolite

DENTAL

Blue Lace Agate, Fluorite, White Agate, Banded Agate, Amazonite, Howlite, Neon Apatite, Rutilated Quartz, Vesuvianite, Lapis Lazuli

DEHYDRATION

Mookaite, Mica, Moss Agate, Aquamarine, Selenite

DEPRESSION

Smoky Quartz, Lapis Lazuli, Rose Quartz, Tiger's Eye, Hematite, Sunstone, Celestite, Mica, Pink Tourmaline, Citrine, Lepidolite, Carnelian, Orange Calcite, Laguna Agate, Amethyst, Red Tiger's Eye

DELUSIONS
Carnelian, Amethyst, Sodalite

DEMENTIA
Blue Chalcedony, Blue Lace Agate, Blue Tiger's Eye

DENIAL
Rhodonite, Rhodochrosite, Amazonite, Crazy Lace Agate

DESPAIR
Lapis Lazuli, Rose Quartz, Lepidolite, Botswana Agate, Rhodochrosite, Turquoise, Rutilated Quartz, Kunzite, Sunstone, Emerald

DETACH AND RELEASE ENTITIES
Selenite, Spirit Quartz, Candle Quartz, Apophyllite, Smoky Quartz, Amethyst, Phantom Quartz, Larimar, Smoky Citrine

DETOX THE BODY
Black Obsidian, Fancy Jasper, Amber, Bloodstone, Carnelian, Lapis Lazuli, Malachite, Snowflake Obsidian, Amethyst, Turquoise, Smoky Quartz, Iolite, Zoisite

DIABETES
Citrine, Pink Opal, Red Jasper, Sodalite, Malachite, Ruby, Black Tourmaline, Pyrite, Bloodstone

DIARRHOEA
Malachite, Tiger'seye, Green Tourmaline, Lapis Lazuli, Serpentine, Honey Calcite

DIGESTION
Citrine, Moss Agate, Jasper, Tiger's Eye, Yellow Aventurine, Banded Agate, Bloodstone, Moss Agate, Amber, Chrysocolla, Rhodonite, Topaz, Malachite, Serpentine, Blue Chalcedony, Jade

DISPEL NEGATIVITY/NEGATIVE ENERGIES

Amethyst, Black Jasper, Black Onyx. Black Tourmaline, Selenite, Smoky Quartz, Snowflake Obsidian, Labradorite, Apache Tears, Bloodstone, Carnelian, Green Tourmaline, Fluorite, Jade, Morganite

DIVINE LOVE

Rose Quartz, Pink Opal, Pink Kunzite, Pink Tourmaline, Angelite, Watermelon Tourmaline, Strawberry Quartz

DIZZINESS

Lapis Lazuli, Malachite, Red Jasper, Amethyst, Black Obsidian, Black Tourmaline, Hematite, Bloodstone, Dioptase, White Sapphire

DNA REPAIR

Herkimer Diamond, Pyrite, Fluorite, Ametrine, Chrysocolla, Garnet

DREAM RECALL/DREAM ENHANCE

Jade, Herkimer Diamond, Kyanite, Smoky Quartz, Amethyst, Ruby, Ametrine, Malachite, Chyrsoprase, Labradorite, Danburite

DYSLEXIA

Black Tourmaline, Sugilite, Malachite, Rose Quartz, Blue Lace Agate, Fluorite

Crystals ailment recipes E
(Combine 3 or more crystals for best outcome)

EAR ACHE/INFECTION
Amethyst, Lapis Lazuli, Rhodonite, Orange Calcite, Amber, Blue Lace Agate, Sodalite, Blue Tiger's Eye

EARTH HEALING
Smoky Quartz, Brown Jasper, Brown Aragonite, Any Brown Stones, Banded Agate, Tiger's Eye, Miriam Any Black Stones (Though brown are the best for healing earth)

EATING DISORDER
Fluorite, Pink Tourmaline, Carnelian, Tiger's Eye, Rhodonite

ECZEMA
Any Aventurine, Amethyst, Sapphire, Blue Lace Agate, Fuchsite, Lapis Lazuli, Rose Quartz, Aquamarine, Black Tourmaline, Shungite

EGOTISM
Magnesite, Garnet, Snowflake Obsidian, Rose quartz

EMF- ELECTROMAGNETIC FIELD
Sodalite, Black Tourmaline, Amazonite, Smoky Quartz, Red Jasper, Unakite, Mica, Banded Agate, Lepidolite, Shungite

EMOTIONAL ABUSE healing
Rose Quartz, Pink Opal, Rhodochrosite, Pink Carnelian, Pink Tourmaline, Green Aventurine, Green Fluorite, Green Tourmaline

EMOTIONAL BAGGAGE release
Petalite, Rhodonite, Any Pink and Yellow crystals

EMOTIONAL BALANCE
Malachite, Rose Quartz, Moonstone, Rhodochrosite, Garnet, Amethyst, Sodalite, Moss Agate, Rhodonite, Ruby

EMOTIONAL BLOCKAGE
Apache Tears, Black Obsidian, Kyanite, Rose Quartz, Malachite, Moldavite, Kunzite, Any Yellow Stones

EMOTIONAL DEPENDENCY
Lepidolite

EMOTIONAL HEALING
Clear Quartz, Green Aventurine, Jade, Lapis Lazuli, Rose Quartz, Moonstone, Peridot, Amethyst, Angelite, Hematite

EMOTIONAL MANIPULATION
Pink Carnelian, Yellow Aventurine, Peach Aventurine

EMOTIONAL TRAUMA
Aqua Aura, Green Aventurine, Rose Quartz, Amazonite, Charoite, Rhodonite

ENERGY
Increase positivity- Green Aventurine, Chrysoprase, Rose Quartz, Amazonite, Sunstone, Yellow Jasper, Yellow Aventurine

ENDOCRINE SYSTEM
Amber, Tourmaline, Amethyst, Peridot, Fire Agate, Pink Tourmaline, Citrine, Howlite

ENHANCE PSYCHIC ABILITIES

Any Goldstone, Selenite, Labradorite, Celestite, Clear Quartz

ENTITIES release

Spirit Quartz, Fairy Quartz, Amethyst, Larimar, Smoky Quartz

EPILEPSY

Jasper, Kyanite, Selenite, Lapis Lazuli, Sugilite, Any Tourmaline, Black Onyx

EXHAUSTION

Tiger's Eye, Citrine, Lepidolite, Carnelian, Orange Calcite, Turquoise

EYES

General- Aquamarine, Opal, Aqua Aura, Bloodstone, Citrine, Green Aventurine, Tiger's Eye, Labradorite, Lapis Lazuli, Jade, Green Fluorite, Green Tourmaline

Cataract- Turquoise

Disease- Jade, Tiger's eye

Disorder- Jade

Vision- Green Aventurine

Infection- Clear Quartz, Blue Lace Agate, Red Tiger's Eye

Watering- Aquamarine

Soothe- Emerald

Crystals ailment recipes F
(Combine 3 or more crystals for best outcome)

FAINTING

Lapis Lazuli, Amethyst

FACIAL (beauty)

Rose Quartz, Jade, Carnelian, Citrine, Aquamarine, Pink Tourmaline, Rainbow Moonstone, Blue Lace Agate

FACIAL PARALYSIS

Lepidolite, Green Fluorite, Diamond, Kunzite, Moonstone

FAIRIES CONNECTION

Amethyst, Clear Quartz, Blue Lace Agate, Rose Quartz, Fairy Quartz

FAITH

Labradorite, Emerald, Golden Topaz

FALLOPIAN TUBE

Carnelian, Unakite, Chrysoprase, Moonstone

FATIGUE

Blue Opal, Hematite, Ametrine, Carnelian, Pyrite, Citrine, Tiger's Eye, Rose Quartz, Rutilated Quartz, Amethyst, Bloodstone, Dioptase

FATS

Iolite, Blue Apatite, Yellow Apatite, Carnelian

FEAR

Sodalite, Orange Calcite, Tiger's Eye, Amethyst, Citrine, Smoky Quartz, Amazonite, Angelite, Pink Tourmaline, Black Tourmaline, Aquamarine

FEET

Onyx, Pyrite, Smoky Quartz, Brown Jasper, Mahagony Obsidian, Dalmatian Jasper, Leopard Skin Jasper, Jet

FERTILITY

Rose Quartz, Moonstone, Carnelian, Unakite, Amber, Garnet, Jade, Ruby in Zoisite

FEVER

Sodalite, Fuchsite, Green Calcite, Larimar, Blue Lace Agate, Chrysoprase, Peridot, Aquamarine

FIBROMYALGIA

Amethyst, Rose Quartz, Citrine, Carnelian, Orange Calcite

FINGER NAIL strengthen

Calcite, Blue Lace Agate

FIRST AID

Fall- Amethyst

Stop bleeding- Bloodstone

Panic- Hematite

Calmness- Rose Quartz

Cheerfulness- Protection

Protect- Black Tourmaline

FOCUS

Amethyst, Carnelian, Fluorite, Jasper, Green Tourmaline, Snowflake Obsidian, Banded Agate

FORGIVENESS

Rhodochrosite, Rhodonite, Rose Quartz, Sugilite, Chyrsoprase

FLEXIBILITY

Azurite, Selenite, Malachite

FOOD POISONING

Citrine, Emerald

FORGETFULNESS

Moss Agate, Sodalite, Unakite, Rhodonite, Emerald

FORGIVENESS

Chrysoprase, Rhodonite, Sugilite, Rose Quartz, Apache Tear

FRACTURE

Hematite, Fluorite, Malachite, Tiger's Eye, Chrysocolla, Blue Lace Agate

FRIENDSHIP (Strengthen)

Clear Quartz, Rhodonite, Turquoise

FRIGIDITY

Carnelian, Moonstone, Ruby, Rose Quartz, Prehnite, Garnet

FROZEN SHOULDER

Blue Tiger's Eye, Blue Chalcedony

FRUSTRATION

Any Obsidian

Crystals ailment recipes G
(Combine 3 or more crystals for best outcome)

GALL BLADDER
Carnelian, Citrine, Fluorite, Orange Calcite, Amber, Danburite, Peridot, Tiger's eye

GAS
Carnelian, Emerald, Agate, Jasper, Any Yellow Stones

GOAL FULFILL
Tiger's eye, Green Aventurine, Carnelian

GOOD LUCK
Tiger's Eye, Green Aventurine, Sunstone, Goldstone, Blue Goldstone, Jade, Citrine,
Blue Tiger's Eye

GRIEF
Apache Tears, Smoky Quartz, Rose Quartz, Amethyst, Lapis Lazuli, Onyx, Azurite, Red Jasper, Rhodochrosite

GROUNDING
Smoky Quartz, Black Tourmaline, Black Obsidian, Black Onyx, Any Jasper, Pyrite, Agate, Apache Tears, Bloodstone, Hematite, Snowflake Obsidian, Banded Agate, Red Tiger's Eye

GUARDIAN ANGEL

Connects you to angels- Angelite, Labradorite

Enhance connection- Amethyst, Clear Quartz

Crystals ailment recipes H
(Combine 3 or more crystals for best outcome)

HAEMORRHAGE

Cats Eye, Hematite, Ruby, Red Tiger's Eye, Bloodstone

HAEMORRHOIDS

Bloodstone, Hematite, Ruby, Carnelian, Chrysocolla, Ametrine, Ruby, Pearl, Red Jasper, Sapphire

HAIR

Chrysocolla, Larimar, Aquamarine, Tourmaline, Agate

Alopecia- Moonstone

Baldness- Unakite

Stimulate hair growth- Galena, Chalcopyrite

Hair loss- Aragonite

HALLUCINATION

Lapis Lazuli, Blue Chalcedony

HAPPINESS

Citrine, Rose Quartz, Sunstone, Carnelian, Green Aventurine, Moonstone, Pyrite, Ruby, Fuchsite, All Calcites, Prehnite, Aquamarine, Rainbow Quartz, Sunshine Aura Quartz

HARMONY

Amazonite, Amethyst, Aquamarine, Clear Quartz, Hematite, Moonstone, Sunstone, Selenite, Jade, Rhodonite

HEADACHE

Amethyst, Sugilite, Lapis Lazuli, Turquoise, Celestite, Citrine, Smoky Quartz, Aquamarine

HEALING AFTER SURGERY

Amethyst, Clear Quartz, Malachite, Selenite

HEALING CRISIS

Azurite, Moldavite

HEALING THE HEALER

Prehnite, Selenite

HEALING WOUNDS

Rhodonite, Ruby, Mookaite, Garnet, Amber

HEALTH (general)

Clear Quartz, Amber, Amethyst, Green Calcite, Red Jasper, Fluorite, Smoky Quartz, Green Aventurine, Selenite, Jade, Pyrite, Amazonite, Moss Agate

HEART (physical)

Amazonite, Blue Lace Agate, Green Aventurine, Green Calcite, Peridot, Watermelon Tourmaline, Sapphire, Rose Quartz

HEARTACHE

Rose Quartz, Green Aventurine, Pink Tourmaline, Rhodonite, Aquamarine, Chrysocolla, Lepidolite

HEARTBURN

Clear Quartz, Peridot, Green Calcite, Aquamarine, Bloodstone, Citrine, Amethyst, Yellow Aventurine

HEATSTROKE

Blue Lace Agate, Rose Quartz, Aquamarine

HELPLESSNESS

Smoky Quartz, Any Brown Stones, Hematite

HERNIA

Mookaite, Red Jasper, Garnet, Red Tiger's Eye

HERPES

Fluorite, Lapis Lazuli

HIGHER REALMS (connection)

Clear Quartz, Moonstone, Selenite, Labradorite, Celestite, Galaxy Quartz

HOPE

Moss Agate, Yellow Aventurine, Jasper, Green Aventurine

HORMONES

Balance- Moonstone, Labradorite, Carnelian, Chyrsoprase, Watermelon Tourmaline, Ruby

Boosting- Amethyst

Regulate- Watermelon Tourmaline

HOUSE PROTECTION

Black Tourmaline and Selenite placed in each rooms and corners of the house.

HIP PAIN

Smoky Quartz, Jade, Azurite

HYPERTENSION

Rose Quartz, Amethyst, Amazonite

HYSTERIA

Rose Quartz, Moonstone, Crazy Lace Agate, Blue Lace Agate, Lapis Lazuli, Turquoise, Topaz, Amethyst

Crystals ailment recipes I
(Combine 3 or more crystals for best outcome)

IDLENESS

Garnet, Aquamarine, Obsidian

ILLNESS (multiple issues)

Moonstone, Fluorite, Banded Agate, Bloodstone, Hematite

IMMUNE SYSTEM BOOST

Amethyst, Malachite, Lapis Lazuli, Moss Agate, Clear Quartz, Bloodstone, Fuchsite, Carnelian, Moonstone, Ametrine, Lepidolite, Mookaite

IMMUNE SYSTEM STRENGTHEN

Bloodstone, Lapis, Malachite, Ametrine, Black Tourmaline, Green Tourmaline, Brown Jasper, Mookaite, Turquoise, Ruby in Zoisite

IMPOTENCE

Carnelian, Moonstone, Garnet, Variscite, Sodalite

INCREASE METABOLISM

Citrine, Labradorite, Tiger's Eye, Yellow Jasper, Yellow Aventurine, Honey Calcite, Copper, Sodalite

INCREASE POSITIVE ENERGY
Green Aventurine, Sunstone, Rose Quartz, Citrine, Amazonite

INDIGESTION
Peridot, Citrine, Yellow Aventurine, Yellow Jasper, Honey Calcite, Tiger's Eye

INFECTION
Blue Lace Agate, Carnelian, Green Fluorite, Selenite, Malachite, Turquoise, Moss Agate, Banded Agate, Bloodstone

INFERTILITY
Moonstone, Carnelian, Rainbow Moonstone, Garnet, Amber

INFLAMMATION
Pyrite, Blue Lace Agate, Malachite, Aventurine, Bloodstone, Blue Chalcedony, Larimar

INFLEXIBILITY
Aquamarine, Citrine, Moonstone

INJURY
Clear Quartz, Red Jasper, Amethyst, Malachite, Rose Quartz, Moonstone, Hematite, Obsidian

INNER CHILD
Amethyst, Clear Quartz, Aquamarine, Rose Quartz, Fuchsite

INSECT BITES
Rhodonite

INSECURITY
Red Jasper, Black Tourmaline, Black Obsidian, Smoky Quartz, Agate

INSOMNIA
Amethyst, Lapis Lazuli, Sodalite, Smoky Quartz, Selenite, Moonstone, Hematite, Aquamarine, Howlite, Zoisite

INSPIRATION

Aquamarine, Citrine, Emerald, Ruby, Fuchsite

INTESTINES

Carnelian, Garnet, Yellow Jasper, Ruby, Peridot, Yellow Aventurine, Green Aventurine, Citrine, Petalite, Snowflake Obsidian

INTUITION

Amethyst, Lapis Lazuli, Moonstone, Sodalite, Tiger's Eye, Labradorite, Purple Fluorite, Selenite, Sugilite, Clear Quartz, Blue Tiger's Eye

IRRITABILITY

Jade, Amethyst, Rhodonite, Bloodstone, Apatite

IRRITABLE BOWEL

Orange Calcite, Bloodstone, Citrine, Yellow Aventurine, Green Aventurine

ITCHING

Amethyst, Malachite, Azurite, Hematite

Crystals ailment recipes J
(Combine 3 or more crystals for best outcome)

JAUNDICE

Ametrine, Yellow Sapphire

JEALOUSY

Rhodochrosite, Amethyst, Peridot

JETLAG

Black Tourmaline, Onyx

JOB INTERVIEW

Citrine, Aventurine, Ruby, Tiger's eye, Jade, Sunstone

JOINTS

Pain- Black Obsidian, Malachite, Orange Calcite, Hematite, Snowflake Obsidian, Lepidolite, Aragonite

Inflammation- Hematite, Lapis Lazuli

Strengthening- Calcite

JOY

Amazonite, Citrine, Clear Quartz, Rose Quartz, Sunstone, Sugilite, Jade, Lemon Topaz

Crystals ailment recipes K
(Combine 3 or more crystals for best outcome)

KARMA/KARMIC ISSUES

Blue Fluorite, Lapis Lazuli, Emerald, Fuchsite, Rainbow Aura

KIDNEY

Bloodstone, Carnelian, Citrine, Clear Quartz, Fluorite, Hematite, Jade, Rose Quartz, Ruby, Fuchsite, Sunstone, Smoky Quartz, Yellow Jasper, Nephrite, Chrysocolla

KNEE

Black Obsidian, Blue Lace Agate, Azurite, Hematite

KUNDALINI RISE

Cinnabar, Moldavite, Serpentine

Crystals ailment recipes L
(Combine 3 or more crystals for best outcome)

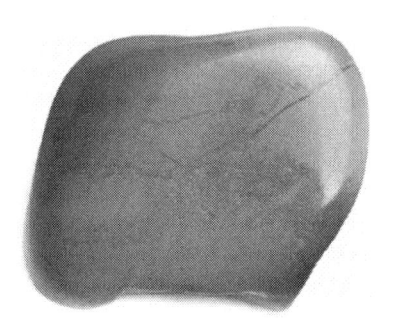

LABOR PAIN

Malachite, Rainbow Moonstone, Carnelian, Hematite, Aquamarine, Smoky Quartz

LACTATION

Malachite + Rainbow Moonstone, Chalcedony, Jade

LAUGHTER

Crazy Lace Agate, Carnelian, Sunstone, Rose Quartz

LAZINESS

Carnelian, Ruby, Red jasper, Obsidian

LEARNING DIFFICULTIES

Sugilite

LEGS PROBLEM

Garnet, Aquamarine, Red Jasper, Ruby, Fuchsite, Smoky Quartz, Bloodstone, Blue Tiger's Eye

LETHARGY

Tourmaline, Red Jasper, Ruby, Ametrine, Red Tiger's Eye

LEUKAEMIA

Garnet, Hematite, Bloodstone, Alexandrite

LIGAMENTS torn

Stibilite

LIGHT HEADEDNESS

Amethyst, Sodalite, Ametrine

LIVER

Amazonite, Bloodstone, Garnet, Emerald, Carnelian, Jade, Malachite, Peridot, Fuchsite, Sodalite, Sunstone, Citrine, Amethyst, Azurite, Danburite, Honey Calcite

LIVER DETOXIFY

Malachite

LONELINESS

Snowflake Obsidian, Calcite, Red Jasper, Rose Quartz, Rhodochrosite, Amethyst, Aquamarine, Onyx, Garnet

LOVE

Rose Quartz, Green Aventurine, Rhodochrosite, Fuchsite, Amethyst, Sugilite, Pink Tourmaline, Pink Opal, Jade

LOW SELF-ESTEEM

Amethyst, Sodalite, Carnelian, Citrine

LUNGS

Amethyst, Aventurine, Chrysocolla, Lapis Lazuli, Peridot, Kunzite, Turquoise, Serpentine, Watermelon Tourmaline, Pink Tourmaline, Petalite

LUST control

Onyx

Crystals ailment recipes M
(Combine 3 or more crystals for best outcome)

MANIFESTATION

Carnelian, Citrine, Green Aventurine, Rainbow Fluorite, Sugilite, Topaz, Aquamarine

MALARIA

Blue Lace Agate, Turquoise, Lapis Lazuli, Iolite

MAXIMIZE ENERGY FLOW

Citrine, Clear Quartz, Selenite

MEDITATION

Amethyst, Golden Calcite, Kyanite, Clear Quartz, Selenite, Ametrine, Blue Lace Agate, Lapis Lazuli, Sugilite, Sodalite

MEDITATION state reached easily

Amethyst, Celestite, Larimar, Labradorite, Selenite, Clear Quartz

MEMORY BOOST

Pyrite, Clear Quartz, Rhodonite, Fluorite, Amethyst, Carnelian, Banded Agate, Amber, Unakite

MEMORIES painful

Rhodonite, Rose Quartz, Clear Quartz, Amazonite, Sodalite

MENOPAUSE

Moonstone, Garnet, Ruby, Carnelian, Amber, Cinnabar, Pearl, Zincite, Diamond, Rhodochrosite, Chrysoprase

MENSTRUATION

Irregular- Red Jasper

Bring- Wulfenite

Excess- Carnelian + Red Jasper

Cramps- Pearl, Chrysocolla, Citrine, Lapis Lazuli

Regulate- Moonstone + Carnelian

MENSTRUAL MOOD SWINGS

Lapis Lazuli, Moonstone, Unakite, Rose Quartz

MENTAL FOCUS & CLARITY

Fluorite, Citrine, Clear Quartz, Ametrine, Amazonite, Tiger's Eye, Sodalite

Mental breakdown- Rhodonite, Smithsonite

Mental burden- Amethyst

Mental disease- Tiger's eye

MERIDIANS

Larimar, Clear Quartz, Tourmaline

METABOLISM stimulate

Sodalite, Amazonite, Labradorite, Fire Agate, Goldstone, Apatite, Red Carnelian, Red Tiger's Eye

MIGRAINE

Lapis Lazuli, Amethyst, Amber, Malachite, Mica, Dioptase, Magnesite

MID-LIFE CRISIS
Rose Quartz
MIND CHATTER
Amethyst, Lapis Lazuli, Selenite, Amazonite, Turquoise, Aquamarine, Zircon, Blue Sapphire
MISCARRIAGE healing
Wulfenite
MOOD SWINGS
Moonstone, Moss Agate, Mica
MOON MANIFESTATION
Moonstone, Clear Quartz, Selenite. (Other stones to be used as per your wish to be manifested)
MOTION SICKNESS
Lapis Lazuli, Rose Quartz, Malachite
MOTIVATION
Citrine, Carnelian, Ruby, Red Tiger's Eye, Amethyst, Rutilated Quartz
MOUTH
Apatite, Lapis Lazuli, Rose Quartz, Apophyllite, Tiger's Eye, Sodalite, Rhodonite
MUSCLE PAIN
Amazonite, Chrysocolla, Hematite, Snowflake Obsidian
Cramps- Bloodstone, Selenite, Tourmaline, Apache Tear
Flexibility- Fuchsite
Soreness- Kyanite, Turquoise, Tourmaline
Spasm- Red Tiger's Eye, Chrysocolla, Lodestone, Red Tourmaline, Amazonite
Strengthen- Apatite, Peridot, Tourmaline

MULTIPLE SCLEROSIS

Red jasper, Rhodonite, Carnelian, Lapis Lazuli, Rose Quartz

Crystals ailment recipes N
(Combine 3 or more crystals for best outcome)

NAILS

Rhodochrosite, Calcite, Blue Lace Agate

NAUSEA

Yellow Jasper, Yellow Aventurine, Sapphire, Emerald, Citrine, Green Fluorite, Red Aventurine, Dioptase

NATURE CONNECT

Green Tourmaline, Tree Agate, Moss Agate

NECK

Rose Quartz, Lapis Lazuli, Sodalite, Blue Tiger's Eye, Aquamarine, Larimar

NEGATIVITY REMOVAL/PROTECTION

Amazonite, Aqua Aura, Black Tourmaline, Citrine, Fluorite, Hematite, Black Obsidian, Grey Jasper, Fire Agate, Snowflake Obsidian, Amethyst, Tiger's Eye, Red Tiger's Eye, Blue Tiger's Eye, Carnelian

NERVE DAMAGE

Kunzite, Selenite

NERVES

Amethyst, Amazonite, Smoky Quartz, Fluorite, Jade, Pink Tourmaline

NERVOUSNESS

Watermelon Tourmaline, Sapphire, Amethyst, Lapis Lazuli, Rhodochrosite

NEW BEGINNINGS

Moss Agate, Moonstone, Kyanite, Rose Quartz, Blue Tiger's Eye, Green Aventurine

NIGHTMARES

Amethyst, Pink Calcite, Smoky Quartz, Ruby, Turquoise, Jasper, Fuchsite, Topaz

NOSE BLEED

Carnelian, Sodalite

NOSE PROBLEMS

Magnetite, Sodalite, Blue Chalcedony, Blue Lace Agate, Lapis Lazuli

NUTRIENT ABSORPTION

Fluorite, Turquoise, Serpentine, Pietersite

Crystals ailment recipes O
(Combine 3 or more crystals for best outcome)

OBESITY

Black Tourmaline, Black Obsidian, Apatite, Iolite, Citrine, Tiger's Eye, Carnelian, Zircon, Honey Calcite

OCD- OBSESSIVE COMPULSIVE DISORDER

Lapis lazuli, Amethyst, Onyx

OPPORTUNITIES

Blue Tiger's Eye, Green Aventurine

OPTIC NERVE

Phenacite, Green Aventurine Citrine, Amethyst, Malachite

OPTIMISM

Citrine, Sunstone

OSTEOPOROSIS

Angelite, Howlite, Malachite, Blue Fluorite, Amazonite, Larimar, Hematite

OVARIAN CANCER

Rhodochrosite

OVARIES

Amber, Onyx, Carnelian, Topaz, Orange Calcite, Peach Aventurine, Chrysoprase, Unakite, Red Aventurine

OVERACTIVE MIND

Sodalite, Aquamarine, Amethyst, Kyanite, Fluorite

OVER-SENSITIVE

Rose Quartz, Green Aventurine, Sodalite

OVERWHELMED

Amethyst, Aquamarine, Jade, Rose Quartz

Crystals ailment recipes P
(Combine 3 or more crystals for best outcome)

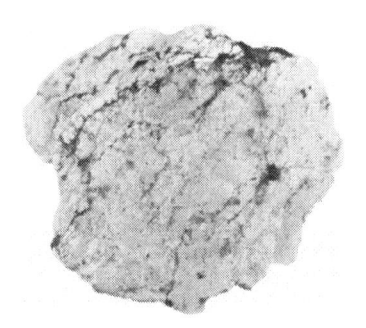

PAIN RELIEF

Rose Quartz, Malachite, Lapis Lazuli, Amethyst, Sugilite, Hematite, Boji Stone, Larimar, Seraphinite

PANCREAS

Bloodstone, Blue Lace Agate, Carnelian, Garnet, Citrine, Moonstone, Turquoise, Smoky Quartz, Topaz, Banded Agate, Chrysocolla

PANIC ATTACKS

Turquoise, Kunzite, Rhodonite, Sodalite, Lapis Lazuli, Pink Tourmaline

PARALYSIS

Amethyst, Emerald, Watermelon Tourmaline, Sapphire

PARANOIA

Rhodochrosite

PARASITES

Amethyst, Rutilated Quartz, Serpentine

PARATHYROID

Lapis Lazuli, Blue Kyanite, Blue Chalcedony

PARKINSON DISEASE
Opal, Opalite, Rose Quartz, Celestite
PASSION
Ruby, Rose Quartz, Garnet, Red Jasper
PAST- letting go
Rutilated Quartz, Smoky Quartz, Citrine
PAST LIFE
Recall- Petrified Wood, Amber, Apatite, Selenite, Rutilated Quartz
Addiction- Iolite
Betrayal- Rhodonite
Broken Heart- Rose Quartz, Rhodonite
Blockages- Lepidolite
Curses- Tiger's Eye, Black Tourmaline
PATIENCE
Howlite, Amber, Labradorite
PCOS
Moonstone, Carnelian, Unakite, Amber, Orange Calcite
PEACE
Rose Quartz, Amethyst, Turquoise, Blue Lace Agate, Celestite, Sugilite, Angelite, Jade
PERSONALITY DISORDER
Tiger's Eye
PHOBIAS
Rose Quartz, Aquamarine, Citrine, Smoky Quartz, Sodalite
PHYSICAL STRENGTH
Red Jasper, Hematite, Ruby
PILES

Bloodstone, Red jasper, Ametrine, Ruby, Chrysocolla, Red Tiger's Eye

PINEAL GLAND

Amethyst, Clear Quartz, Fuchsite, Opal, Ruby

PITUITARY GLAND

Amethyst, Garnet, Moonstone, Opal, Iolite

PLANTS

Tree Agate, Moss Agate

PMS

Moonstone, Rose Quartz, Ruby, Selenite, Opal

PNEUMONIA

Fluorite, Sodalite

POSITIVE THINKING/ENERGY

Pyrite, Sunstone, Black Tourmaline, Smoky Quartz, Rose Quartz, Green Aventurine,
Selenite

PREGNANCY PHASE

Moonstone, Red Jasper, Unakite, Jade, Lapis Lazuli, Rose Quartz, Carnelian

PROTECTION

Black Tourmaline, Black Obsidian, Turquoise, Onyx, Smoky Quartz, Citrine, Tiger's Eye, Red Jasper, Grey Jasper, Fire Agate, Carnelian, Lapis Lazuli, Labradorite, Pyrite, Amethyst, Jade, Snowflake Obsidian

PROTECTION AGAINST WITCHCRAFT/BLACK MAGIC

Red Jasper and Black Tourmaline together

PROTECTION Aura

Labradorite, Aquamarine, Black Tourmaline, Lapis Lazuli, Selenite

PROTECTION DURING PSYCHIC WORK

Yellow Jasper, Snowflake Obsidian, Smoky Quartz

PROSPERITY

Citrine, Moss Agate, Ruby, Jade, Green Aventurine, Sunstone, Amethyst, Bloodstone, Cinnabar, Green Tourmaline, Peridot, Pyrite, Petrified Wood, Goldstone

PROSTATE

Red Jasper, Selenite, Chrysoprase, Obsidian, Chrysocolla

PSORIASIS

Amethyst, Blue Lace Agate, Labradorite, Selenite, Yellow Agate, Banded Agate

PSYCHIC ABILITIES enhance

Clear Quartz, Labradorite, Selenite, Celestite, Galaxy Quartz, Sodalite, Sugilite, Herkimer Diamond, Opal, Fluorite

PSYCHIC COMMUNICATION

Any Goldstone, Clear Quartz

PSYCHIC PROTECTION/ATTACK

Apache Tears, Ruby, Black Tourmaline, Aqua Aura, Black Obsidian, Black Tourmaline, Lapis Lazuli, Labradorite, Selenite, Howlite, Citrine, Blue Tiger's Eye, Red Tiger's Eye

PUBERTY

Green Aventurine, Jade, Citrine, Moonstone, Opal

PUS

Bloodstone

Crystals ailment recipes R
(Combine 3 or more crystals for best outcome)

RAGE

Amethyst, Carnelian, Green Aventurine, Howlite, Jade, Rose Quartz, Sugilite

RASHES

Bloodstone, Hematite, Ruby, Rhyolite

RECOVERY (quick)

Ruby in Zoisite

RED BLOOD CELLS

Amethyst, Hematite, Bloodstone, Any RED Stones

REDUCE ACCIDENTS

Amethyst, Turquoise, Tiger's Eye, Smoky Quartz

REGULATE BLOOD PRESSURE

Sodalite, Green Aventurine, Amazonite, Green Calcite

REJUVENATION

Sodalite, Citrine, Rhodonite, Lapis Lazuli

RELAXATION

Amethyst, Pink Tourmaline, Gold Calcite, Smoky Quartz, Rose Quartz, Red Jasper, Green Aventurine, Fuchsite, Dioptase, Peridot

RELEASE OLD HABIT/PATTERN/ISSUES

Moss Agate, Aquamarine

REMOVE KARMIC HOOKS

Orange Calcite

REPRESSED ANGER

Lapis Lazuli, Amethyst, Rhodonite

REPRODUCTIVE ORGANS

Carnelian, Rhodochrosite, Ruby, Fuchsite, Unakite, Amber

RESCUE REMEDY

Larimar + Rhodochrosite + Rhodonite

RESENTMENT

Smoky Quartz, Peridot

RHEUMATISM

Amber, Carnelian, Fluorite, Malachite, Turquoise, Chrysocolla, Azurite

RIGHT USE OF WILL

Carnelian, Sunstone

RINGWORM

Calcite, Zircon

Crystals ailment recipes S
(Combine 3 or more crystals for best outcome)

SADNESS

Azurite, Red Jasper, Sodalite, Ruby, Rose Quartz

SCHIZOPHRENIA

Tiger's Eye, Ruby, Lepidolite, Blue Obsidian, Sugilite

SCIATICA

Green Tourmaline, Hematite, Rose Quartz, Lepidolite, Kunzite

SELF-ACCEPTANCE

Mango Calcite

SELF-CONTROL

Rutilated Quartz, Amethyst

SELF-ESTEEM

Amazonite, Ametrine, Blue Opal, Carnelian, Garnet, Citrine, Hematite, Lapis Lazuli, Pink Tourmaline, Sodalite, Moss Agate, Red Tiger's Eye

SELF-HATRED

Rutilated Quartz, Rose Quartz

SELF-HEALING

Serpentine, Seraphinite, Larimar, Sunstone

SELF-LOVE

Rose Quartz, Rhodochrosite, Rhodonite

SELF-WORTH

Calcite, Chrysoberyl

SEX DRIVE BALANCE

Red Jasper, Garnet, Red Tiger's Eye

SEX DRIVE increase

Carnelian, Red Jasper, Fire Quartz, Sunstone, Shiva Lingam, Garnet, Rose Quartz, Roselite, Pink Spinel

SEXUAL ABUSE healing

Rhodochrosite, Rhodonite, Pink Carnelian, Pink Tourmaline, Ruby

SEXUALLY TRANSMITTED DISEASE

Malachite, Ruby

SHOULDERS

Blue Lace Agate, Blue Tiger's Eye, Larimar, Blue Chalcedony

SHYNESS

Orange Calcite, Hematite, Malachite, Tiger's Eye

SINUS

Fluorite, Green Aventurine, Emerald, Aquamarine, Sodalite, Blue Tiger's Eye, Bloodstone, Carnelian, Citrine, Smithsonite

SKIN

Amber, Amethyst, Aquamarine, Malachite, Rose Quartz, Ruby, Fuchsite, Snowflake Obsidian, Citrine, Bloodstone, Moonstone

SLEEP (insomnia)

Amethyst, Angelite, Celestite, Clear Quartz, Lapis lazuli, Mica, Selenite
SLEEPWALK
Moonstone, Topaz
SMOKING
Fairy Cross, Amethyst, Kunzite, Labradorite, Peridot, Hematite, Brown Jasper
SORE THROAT
Amber, Blue Topaz, Aquamarine, Blue Lace Agate, Blue Tiger's Eye
SPASMS
Amazonite, Green Aventurine, Azurite, Ruby, Aragonite
SPELLS PROTECTION (against)
Black Tourmaline, Smoky Quartz, Tiger's Eye
SPINE
Selenite, Fuchsite, Blue Tiger's Eye, Garnet, Beryl
SPIRITUAL AWAKENING
Purple Fluorite, Selenite, Clear Quartz, Labradorite, Aqua Aura
SPIRIT GUIDE connect
Angelite, Selenite, Celestite, Kyanite, Amethyst, Lapis Lazuli, Clear Quartz, Smoky Quartz, Amazonite
SPIRITUAL GROWTH
Moonstone, Snowflake Obsidian, Amazonite, Sodalite, Labradorite, Celestite, Clear Quartz
SPLEEN
Amber, Citrine, Fluorite, Peridot, Aquamarine, Chalcedony. Red Obsidian
SPONDYLITIS

Labradorite

STAMINA

Banded Agate, Amethyst, Carnelian, Moonstone

STOMACH ISSUES

Citrine, Fancy Jasper, garnet, Labradorite, Moonstone, Sunstone, Yellow Jasper, Green Aventurine, Chrysocolla, Serpentine

STOMACH UPSET

Emerald, Yellow Jasper, Moonstone, Sunstone, Yellow Aventurine, Citrine, Aquamarine

STOP NEGATIVE VIBRATIONS

Aqua aura, Black Tourmaline, Snowflake Obsidian

STRENGTHEN BONES

Fluorite, Selenite, Peridot, Hematite, Smoky Quartz

STRENGTHEN LEGS

Black Onyx, Peridot, Red Jasper, Picture Jasper

STRESS

Amethyst, Rose Quartz, Labradorite, Black Tourmaline, Green Aventurine, Red Jasper, Lapis Lazuli, Mica, Smoky Quartz, Blue Tiger's Eye, Aquamarine

SUBCONSCIOUS BLOCKS

Malachite, Chrysocolla, Chrysoprase

SUCCESS

Red Tiger's Eye, Citrine, Green Aventurine

SUICIDAL THOUGHTS

Citrine, Lapis Lazuli, Rose Quartz, Snowflake Obsidian, Amber

SUNBURN

Moonstone, Rose Quartz, Angelite, Aquamarine, Blue Lace Agate

SWELLING

Amethyst, Aquamarine, Moonstone, Jet, Malachite

SWOLLEN GLANDS

Bloodstone, Carnelian, Moonstone

Crystals ailment recipes T
(Combine 3 or more crystals for best outcome)

TELEPATHY

Angelite, Clear Quartz, Labradorite, Blue Tiger's Eye

TEMPERATURE balance

Blue Chalcedony

TENSION

Herkimer Diamond, Amethyst, Kunzite, Rose Quartz, Carnelian, Sodalite

THROAT ISSUES

Lapis, Sodalite, Blue Tiger's Eye, Blue Lace Agate, Blue Chalcedony, Larimar, Blue Kyanite

THROMBOSIS

Magnesite

THYMUS (higher heart)

Amethyst, Green Tourmaline, Aqua Aura, Blue Tourmaline, Jadeite, Rose Quartz, Green aventurine, Angelite, Dioptase, Peridot, Smithsonite

THYROID

Aquamarine, Lapis Lazuli, Banded Agate, Amazonite, Citrine, Clear Quartz, Garnet, Sodalite, Blue Tiger's Eye, Blue Lace Agate, Turquoise

TIREDNESS

Pyrite, Amethyst, Fire Agate, Mahogany Obsidian

TISSUES REGENERATE

Citrine, Hematite, Peridot, Unakite, Carnelian

TOBACCO ADDICTION

Hematite

TONSILITIS

Amber, Blue Lace Agate, Sodalite

TOOTH ACHE

Amethyst, Fluorite, Malachite, Lapis Lazuli, Blue Tiger's Eye, Sodalite, Azurite, Blue Onyx, Turquoise

TOXINS

Bloodstone, Malachite, Emerald, Ametrine, Iolite, Beryl

TRAVEL COMBO

Fear and Anxiety- Sodalite

Tiredness/Jetlag- Black Tourmaline

Sleep peacefully- Rose Quartz

Protection- Smoky Quartz

Energy Cleanse- Clear Quartz

TRAVEL SAFETY

Amethyst, Red Jasper, Yellow Jasper, Red Tiger Eye, Blue Tiger's Eye, Moonstone

TRAVEL SICKNESS

Red Jasper, Sodalite, Malachite

TRUST

Sodalite, Pink Calcite, Carnelian, Moss Agate

TUBERCULOSIS

Amber, Blue Sapphire, Morganite, Topaz

TUMORS

Amethyst, Bloodstone, Malachite, Selenite, Smoky Quartz, Petalite, Sapphire

Crystals ailment recipes U
(Combine 3 or more crystals for best outcome)

ULCERS

Ametrine, Fluorite, Rhodonite, Ruby, Fuschite, Selenite, Moonstone, Chrysocolla, Calcite

UNCONDITIONAL LOVE

Rose Quartz, Rhodochrosite, Rhodonite, Kunzite, Pink Tourmaline, Pink Opal

UNDERSTANDING DEATH

Carnelian, Smoky Quartz

UNGROUNDEDNESS

Smoky Quartz, Hematite, Garnet, Boji Stones, Any Black and Brown Stones

UNITY

Clear Quartz, Garnet

URINARY AILMENTS

Banded Agate, Blue Lace Agate, Carnelian, Ruby, Fuchsite, Red Jasper, Banded Agate, Blue Aventurine

URINARY TRACK INFECTION
Carnelian, Orange Calcite
UTERUS
Red Jasper, Pink Tourmaline, Amber, Wulfenite

Crystals ailment recipes V
(Combine 3 or more crystals for best outcome)

VAGINA issues

Carnelian, Orange Calcite

VAMPIRES (energy)

Green Tourmaline, Ruby, Labradorite, Black tourmaline, Aventurine, Smoky Quartz

VARICOSE VEINS

Snowflake Obsidian, Smithsonite, Tourmalines, Amber, Aquamarine, Blue Lace Agate

VEINS

Smithsonite, Snowflake Obsidian

VERTIGO

Lapis Lazuli, Rose Quartz, Malachite, Clear Quartz, Red Jasper, Morganite

VIRAL INFECTIONS

Pyrite, Amethyst, Fluorite, Bloodstone, Carnelian, Turquoise

VISION (eyes)

Citrine (place on eyelids for 20 minutes)

Yellow Aventurine, red Tiger's Eye, Sodalite, Clear Quartz, Fluorite, Topaz, Sapphire

VISUALIZATION

Iolite, Imperial Topaz, Green Tourmaline, Amethyst, Angelite, Blue Kyanite, Celestite

VOMITTING

Citrine, Emerald, Lapis lazuli, Moonstone, Yellow Aventurine

Crystals ailment recipes W
(Combine 3 or more crystals for best outcome)

WARTS

Blue Lace Agate, Labradorite, Smoky Quartz, Calcite, Emerald

WATER PURIFIER

Lithium Quartz

WATER RETENTION

Angelite, Aquamarine, Moonstone, Sodalite, Mookaite

WEAKNESS

Amethyst, Carnelian, Emerald, Hematite, Red jasper, Clear Quartz

WEIGHT CONTROL

Apatite

WEIGHT LOSS

Blue Apatite, Green Tourmaline, Angelite, Kyanite, Citrine, Sunstone, Tiger's Eye, Honey Calcite, Iolite, Unakite, Amethyst

WILL POWER

Tiger's Eye, Garnet, Onyx, Fire Agate, Pyrite, hematite, Rose Quartz, Red Tiger's Eye, Blue Tiger's Eye

WISDOM

Jade, Lapis Lazuli, Carnelian, Amethyst

WORK/WORKPLACE

Rise in pay- Citrine

Banish jealousy- Black Onyx, Black tourmaline, Black Obsidian

Promotion- Green Aventurine

Being artistic- Sodalite

Steady flow of customers- Tiger's Eye

Concentrate, No day-dreaming- Hematite

Confidence, Memory- Carnelian

Overcome obstacles- Aquamarine

WORRY

Amazonite, Red Jasper, Smoky Quartz, Rose Quartz, Jade

WRINKLES

Rose Quartz, Selenite, Fluorite

Zodiacs and Crystals
(Combine 3 or more crystals for best outcome)

These are some of the compatible stones for zodiacs signs; these are not Birthstones.

AQUARIUS (January 20- February 18)

Hematite, Snow Quartz, Clear Quartz, Garnet, Fuchsite, Amethyst, Silver, Aquamarine

PISCES (February 19- March 20)

Rose Quartz, Blue lace Agate, Bloodstone, Clear Quartz, Amethyst, Fluorite, Turquoise, Aquamarine

ARIES (March 21- April 19)

Apache Tears, Red Jasper, Hematite, Clear Quartz, Aventurine, Bloodstone, Citrine, Jade, Turquoise, Amethyst

TAURUS (April 20- May 20)

Red Jasper, Rose Quartz, Clear Quartz, Carnelian, Rhodonite, Iolite, Jade, Selenite, Clear Quartz

GEMINI (May 21- June 20)

Citrine, Apatite, Dalmation Jasper, Howalite, Celestite, Jade, Clear Quartz, Tree Agate, Clear Quartz

CANCER- (June 21- July 22)

Carnelian, Clear Quartz, Moss Agate Moonstone, Opal, Aura Quartz, Calcite, Fire Opal, Ruby

LEO (July 23- August 22)

Labradorite, Carnelian, Rose Quartz, Citrine, Clear Quartz, Amber, Red Jasper, Onyx, Peridot, Sunstone, Rutilated Quartz

VIRGO (August 23- September 22)

Amazonite, Amethyst, Bloodstone, Snowflake Obsidian, Moss Agate, Pink Opal, Sugilite, Clear Quartz

LIBRA (September 23- October 22)

Clear Quartz, Citrine, Bloodstone, Moonstone, Rose Quartz, Aqua Aura, Tourmalines, Opalite, Opal

SCORPIO (October 23- November 22)

Labradorite, Unakite, Moonstone, Clear Quartz, Malachite, Rhodochrosite, Turquoise

SAGGITARIUS (November 23- December 21)

Lapis Lazuli, Smoky Quartz, Sodalite, Labradorite, Herkimer Diamond, Turquoise, Topaz, Clear Quartz

CAPRICORN (December 22- January 19)

Snowflake Obsidian, Tiger's Eye, Smoky Quartz, Rose Quartz, Amethyst, Fluorite, Clear Quartz

How to use the above combination of zodiac stones-

1. Put under pillow

2. Make elixir/ crystal water

3. Make combination bracelet, earring or necklace

4. Use single stone as pendants

5. Keep near your aura

6. Meditate with crystals

7. Make your personal zodiac crystal grid

Beauty Combo
(Combine 3 or more crystals for best outcome)

SKIN- ANTI-AGE
Opal, Blue Lace Agate, Aquamarine, Turquoise, Rose Quartz, Bloodstone, Amber, Ruby, Jade, Malachite, Amethyst, Topaz, Moonstone, Jasper, Citrine

HEALTHY HAIR
Banded Agate, Chrysocolla, Aquamarine, Howlite, Larimar, Goldstone, Jade, Carnelian, Moonstone, Unakite, Opal, Amethyst, Tourmaline, Lapis, Magnetite, Citrine, Red Agate

HAIR LOSS
Blue Opal, Galena, Moonstone, Chalcopyrite, Sandstone, Aragonite, Citrine

BALDNESS
Selenite, Aragonite, Aquamarine

How to use the above beauty combo?

1. Make elixir/ crystal water and consume or wash your face and hair

2. Make elixir and at regular intervals spray on face and hair

3. Massage directly on skin

4. Put under pillow

5. Charge your creams, shampoo, conditioner and cosmetics with these stones by surrounding your cosmetics with them.

6. Put stones directly in cream, shampoo, conditioner, gel etc bottles

7. Make ice cubes with these stones and massage your face

8. Drop hair combos in water bucket and use that water to wash hair

Elemental Crystals
(Combine 3 or more crystals for best outcome)

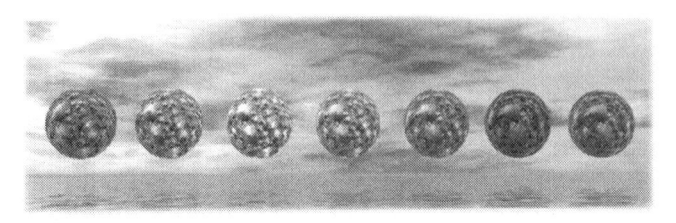

FIRE ELEMENT- Solar Plexus chakra and Sacral chakra

Amber, Garnet, Carnelian, Rhodochrosite, Citrine, Jasper, Orange Calcite, Fire Agate, Lava, Fire Opal, Sunstone, Red Calcite, Sardonyx, Red Tourmaline, Ruby, Labradorite

AIR ELEMENT- Throat chakra and Third Eye chakra

Amethyst, Picture Jasper, Citrine, Sodalite, Blue Calcite, Diamond, Lapis Lazuli, Opal, Nirvana Quartz, Tiger's Eye, Angel Phantom Quartz, Topaz, Zircon, Turquoise, Clear Fluorite

EARTH ELEMENT- Root chakra and Heart chakra

Hematite, Agate, Jade, Celestite, Smoky Quartz, Peridot, Emerald, Obsidian, Green Tourmaline, Onyx, Jasper, Malachite, Jet

WATER ELEMENT- Throat and Heart chakra

Moonstone, Aqua Aura, Fluorite, Aquamarine, Selenite, Azurite, Pearl, Blue Calcite, Blue Tourmaline, Lapis Lazuli, Chalcedony, Chrysocolla

SPIRIT ELEMENT-Crown chakra

Moldavite, Apophyllite, Phenacite, Danburite, Diamond

Some stones belong to multiple elements due to its mixed properties.

Crystals for Soon to Be Moms and New Moms
(Combine 3 or more crystals for best outcome)

LABOR PAIN, LACTATION

Selenite, Rainbow Moonstone, Moonstone, Malachite, Chalcedony, Sodalite

BREAST FEEDING

Moonstone, Milky Quartz, Selenite, Pink Chalcedony,

NAUSEA, DIZZINESS

Snowflake Obsidian, Amethyst, Tiger's eye

DEPRESSION

Aquamarine, Rose Quartz, Citrine

DIGESTION

Chrysocolla, Citrine, Amber

BACKPAIN

Carnelian, Red Jasper, Lava

CALCIUM, HAEMOGLOBIN

Calcite, Hematite, Bloodstone, Red Jasper

ENERGY BOOST, FATIGUE

Carnelian, Rose Quartz, Tiger's Eye, Crazy Lace Agate

SACRAL HEAL

Rainbow Moonstone, Carnelian, Unakite, Amber

STAMINA, RELIEVE PAIN DURING CHILD BIRTH

Black Onyx

HEALING, STRENGTH

Bloodstone

MOTIVATION, COURAGE FOR LABOR

Carnelian

ELIMINATE FEAR

Chrysocolla

RELEASE STRESS

Lapis Lazuli

CLEANSER

Malachite

SOOTHES EMOTIONS

Moonstone

RELEASE BURDEN

Peridot

EMOTIONS, LOVE AND BALANCE

Rose Quartz

ACTIVATES KUNDALINI

Serpentine

How to use the above combos

- Put under pillow at night

- Place in particular room

- Wear in jewelry form

- Make crystal water/elixir

- Put inside manifesting box

- Meditate with crystals

- Make crystal grids for pregnancy or post pregnancy

- Carry with you in pockets

- Make coasters

- As keychains

- Charge your food

Crystals for Furry Babies – Pets

Agate – Calms and relax your pet, balances energy and chakras.

Amber – Flea and ticks.

Amethyst – Master healer, pain, excessive barking, can be used for everything.

Bloodstone – Calms anxiousness, promotes sleep.

Blue Fluorite – Allergies, bones and respiratory system.

Carnelian – Aging pets, allergies, arthritis, cancer, skin issues.

Clear Quartz – Master Healer, can be used for everything.

Citrine – Diabetes, hyperactive, intestine issues, stress, training.

Coral – Bladder, emotional stability, kidney.

Garnet – Reproductive organs.

Green Fluorite – Blood purify lymph and respiratory system.

Hematite – Bounding, grounding, muscular problems.

Jade – Abused, aggression, calms, eyes issues.

Jasper – Digestion. Adding few drops of Jasper elixir to food will help with pet's digestion.

Kyanite – Align all chakras.

Labradorite – Aura protection.

Lapis Lazuli – Pain, respiratory issues.

Moonstone – Bonding, calming, cancer, digestion.

Rose Quartz – Abused pets, aggression, reduces fear and stress, wounds.

Smoky Quartz – Nervous system issues.

Sodalite – Calms your pet, reduces stress, training.

Tiger's eye – Grounding, protection, travel.

Top 12
PSYCHIC ATTACKS

Amethyst
Bloodstone
Black Tourmaline
Black Obsidian
Carnelian
Jasper
Tigers Eye
Lapis Lazuli
Fire Agate
Grey Jasper
Mica
Selenite

GROUNDING

Black Tourmaline
Black Kyanite
Blue Kyanite
Black Obsidian/Onyx
Smoky Quartz
Fire Agate
Dalmatian Jasper
Jasper
Hematite
Agate
Ruby
Carnelian

RELATIONSHIP

Rose Quartz
Morganite
Ruby
Emerald
Rhodochrosite
Malachite
Dioptase
Orange/Red Carnelian
Green Aventurine
Watermelon Tourmaline
Peridot
Moonstone

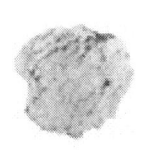

MONEY

Citrine
Green Aventurine
Peridot
Malachite
Pyrite
Jade
Ruby
Tigers Eye
Petrified Wood
Garnet
Carnelian
Cinnabar

WEIGHT LOSS

Blue Apatite
Yellow Apatite
Seraphinite
Bloodstone
Iolite
Carnelian
Citrine
Clear Topaz
Kyanite
Amethyst
Honey Calcite
Tiger's Eye

ANGELIC STONES

Amethyst
Selenite
Angelite
Celestite
Apophyllite
Moldavite
Sugilite
Seraphinite
Prehnite
Clear Quartz
Lemurian
Rainbow Fluorite

TRAVEL

Sodalite
Black Tourmaline
Rose Quartz
Smoky Quartz
Amethyst
Red Jasper
Yellow Jasper
Red Tigers Eye
Blue Tigers Eye
Moonstone
Malachite
Turquoise

Chakras and Crystals

SOUL STAR CHAKRA

Selenite, Clear Quartz, Galaxy Quartz, Milky Quartz

CROWN CHAKRA

Amethyst, Labradorite, Charoite, Selenite, Clear Quartz, Sugilite, Howlite

THIRD EYE CHAKRA

Apophyllite, Sodalite, Pietersite, Selenite, Sapphire, Iolite, Prehnite, Lapis Lazuli

THROAT CHAKRA

Aquamarine, Lapis Lazuli, Turquoise, Blue Lace Agate, Blue Chalcedony, Blue Kyanite

HEART CHAKRA

Green Aventurine, Amazonite, Moldavite, Rose Quartz, Bloodstone, Peridot, Emerald, Dioptase, Rhodochrosite

SOLAR PLEXUS CHAKRA

Amber, Citrine, Yellow Jasper, Honey Calcite, Gold, Tiger's Eye, Golden Topaz, Yellow Aventurine

SACRAL CHAKRA

Wulfenite, Aragonite, Carnelian, Sunstone, Orange Calcite, Pearl, Moonstone

ROOT CHAKRA

Black Tourmaline, Red Jasper, Smoky Quartz, Hematite, Obsidian, Garnet, Jet, Petrified Wood

EARTH STAR CHAKRA

Black Tourmaline, Brown Jasper, Smoky Quartz

About the Author

Rinku Patel is a Reiki Master Teacher, Doreen Virtue Certified-Angel intuitive, Fairyologist, Realm Reader, Crystal healer, Angel card reader, and Indigo card reader. Other than that, she is a Certified Tarot card reader and spiritual writer.

Rinku can be reached via her email address reikithemiraclehealing@gmail.com and on Facebook at **Reiki the Miracle Healing**.

Rinku's book **"The Magic of Crystals in Your Reiki Journey"** is available on **Amazon**.

Printed in Great Britain
by Amazon